T0146908

THE TWELVE
LAWS OF
LEADERSHIP

THE TWELVE LAWS OF LEADERSHIP

For Dentist-Entrepreneurs and Their Executives

DR. MARC B. COOPER

Calligraphy by
Xinyuan Gao (高新元)

 iUniverse®

THE TWELVE LAWS OF LEADERSHIP
FORDENTIST-ENTREPRENEURSANDTHEIREXECUTIVES

iUniverse books may be ordered through booksellers or by contacting:

iUniverse
1663 Liberty Drive
Bloomington, IN 47403
www.iuniverse.com
1-800-Authors (1-800-288-4677)

Because of the dynamic nature of the Internet, any web addresses or links contained in this book may have changed since publication and may no longer be valid. The views expressed in this work are solely those of the author and do not necessarily reflect the views of the publisher, and the publisher hereby disclaims any responsibility for them.

Any people depicted in stock imagery provided by Thinkstock are models, and such images are being used for illustrative purposes only. Certain stock imagery © Thinkstock.

ISBN: 978-1-5320-2684-3 (sc)
ISBN: 978-1-5320-2683-6 (e)

Library of Congress Control Number: 2017910026

Print information available on the last page.

iUniverse rev. date: 10/14/2017

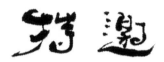

In memory of my parents, Sadie and Sidney
Cooper, who died before they could fully realize
the tremendous contribution they made

A short saying often contains much wisdom.
—Sophocles

ACKNOWLEDGMENTS

How to acknowledge a lifetime of teachers? How do you list the books and articles read, the programs taken, and the relationships cultivated with men and women who have woven their learning into yours? Each contributes a thread to the fabric of the way you see yourself and the world.

Thank you, Werner Erhard, Michael Jensen, Steve Zaffron, Nathen Rosenberg, Neil Mahoney, Ron Bynum, Jim Selman, Heidi Singfield, Alan Cahn, Charlie Smith, Art Haines, Andy Fallat, Joseph Friedman, Dana Carman, Raul Dahl, Daniel Coleman, Joseph Campbell, Robert Mirabal, Stephen Covey, Michael Gerber, Jim Collins, Jerry Porras, Patrick Lencioni, Herta Spencer, Merwyn Landy, David Dinner, Carol Hildebrand, Saul Schluger, Harley Sullivan, Bill Ammons, Beverly Braden, Carl Jung, Abraham Maslow, Edwin Friedman, Murray Bowen, Roshi Susuki, Rabbi Zalman Schachter, Katharine Cahn, Richard Condon, Robert Burch, Jacob Puhl, Damaris Perez, Chris Creamer, Matt King, and Gus Lee.

Thank you Angela Ekstowicz for your assistance and support in readying this book for publication.

Thank you, Landmark Education, Tekniko, Wings Seminars, Pathworks, Naropa University, Neurolinguistic Programing, and the Murray Bowen Centers.

And special thanks to the hundreds of clients over these many years. I have learned from all of you.

Special thanks to Xinyuan Gao for his masterful calligraphy. And, thanks to iUniverse, the publisher, for guiding me through the process and producing this book.

A special acknowledgment goes to my wife, my life partner and best friend, Leslie Copland, who holds me to my highest thought.

INTRODUCTION

This book is intended for dentist-entrepreneurs and their senior executives who are fully committed to growing successfully managed group practices. In my work, I have trained and developed many dentists-entrepreneurs and their senior staff to expand their capacities to go from single or very small group practices to much larger managed group practices. It is my assertion, based on my 30-plus years of client experience and accumulated evidence, the most fundamental and critical element accounting for their success is leadership.

This kind of leadership can generate authentic accountability in partners, associates, staff, and nondentist executives. This leadership leads by influence and not command and control. These sorts of leaders have utmost integrity with their vision, values, and purpose. These leaders can ignite commitment and passion in others and move people past their pettiness, righteousness, and separateness.

Leadership is not some *thing*. It does not have borders, edges, mass, or density. Leadership is neither measurable nor calculable. It has no dimensions and is not quantifiable. If leadership is not a thing, then it is a concept, an abstraction, a human invention to explain an observable phenomenon.

A phenomenon is an exceptional or unusual occurrence. Therefore, leadership is not an ordinary event. It does not happen by default or chance. Leadership is extraordinary, special, and distinct.

The phenomenon of leadership has been described as a leader's speaking and actions resulting in others being inspired, committed, and determined to achieve a future that would not happen anyway.

Leadership has been with us for our entire history, from cavemen to cell phones and from hunter-gatherers to social networking. In fact, every human achievement requires leadership. Therefore, the phenomenon of leadership can be regenerated. Given that it can be regenerated, as is true for any phenomenon that is reproducible, it must obey certain laws for the occurrence to happen.

Just as in the laws of physics, such as the law of gravity, the laws of leadership are immutable and incontrovertible. Laws are independent of human awareness or concern. Laws just are. They don't need to be understood to be operable, but they must be present for the phenomenon to occur. Nevertheless, the more one is aware of the laws of leadership, the more the phenomenon of leadership can be consciously created.

Which laws are inherent to the phenomenon of leadership? Which must be followed for the occurrence of leadership to presence itself?

In my experience of working with many dentist-entrepreneurs and senior executives, I have consistently observed twelve laws that govern leadership. According to numerology, twelve is the number that, when completed, forms a whole, a perfect and harmonious unit. In the ancient civilizations, Asian and Judaic, it corresponds to the plenitude, the completion, and the integrity of a thing. Therefore, all twelve laws of leadership must be in play for leadership to occur.

The twelve laws of leadership are as follows:

- the law of language
- the law of integrity
- the law of context
- the law of responsibility
- the law of self-awareness
- the law of courage
- the law of core values
- the law of authenticity
- the law of intentionality

- the law of vision
- the law of purpose
- the law of contribution

Each chapter presents a fundamental and critical law required for leadership. Each has five sections. One section contains the definition of the word, which is fundamental and critical to the understanding of that law.

Next is a Chinese calligraphy figure representing the title of each law. Chinese characters are logograms used in the writing of Chinese and some other Asian languages. Chinese characters constitute the oldest continuously used system of writing in the world. Given that leadership precedes the written language, we wanted to add another dimension to this book to represent the timelessness of leadership and its required laws.

Following that, the law itself is stated. Then the elements that make up that law are noted. Finally a quote that validates the law is offered.

This book is about distinguishing these twelve laws critical for the phenomenon of leadership to occur. I assert that if you obey these laws, your ability as a leader will be dramatically enhanced.

I suggest you read each law carefully. Ask yourself, *How am I following this law in my leadership? How am I operating in accordance with this law? What have I seen that I have never seen before? What insights am I gaining? To be mindful of this law, what do I need to do, and who do I need to be?*

Acknowledging and understanding these laws will help you be a better leader but will also help you be a better human being—more powerful, more thoughtful, and more connected. And once you begin, this journey of mastering the twelve laws of leadership is now.

Dr. Marc B.
Cooper, President
and Chairman,
DEO Dental
Group Inc.

慎言慎言

THE LAW OF LANGUAGE

THE LAW OF LANGUAGE

Definitions of Language

The words, their pronunciation, and the methods of combining them used and understood by a community

A systematic means of communicating ideas or feelings by the use of conventionalized signs, sounds, gestures, or marks having understood meanings

The Law of Language

Language is superior ordinate.

Elements of the Law of Language

You belong to language.

You don't have language; it has you.

Language gives you your world.

Language determines what and how you perceive.

Leaders speak the language of the future.

Leaders speak about a future that is possible.

Leaders deeply feel the words they speak.

Honor language as the cause.

The limits of my language means
the limits of my world.

—Ludwig Wittgenstein

THE LAW OF INTEGRITY

THE LAW OF INTEGRITY

Definitions of Integrity

Whole; complete; nothing left out

Adherence to a code of values

An unimpaired condition; soundness

The quality or state of being complete or undivided

The Law of Integrity

Without integrity, nothing works.

Elements of the Law

Keep your word.

Be your word.

Your word is your vow.

Your word gives you who you are.

Honor yourself as your word to build trust, affinity, and commitment.

When you don't keep your word, clean up the mess you've made.

Holding integrity as the central core value creates a culture of success.

Obey the law of integrity; results will follow.

In looking for people to hire, you look for three qualities: integrity, intelligence, and energy. And if they don't have the first, the other two will kill you.

—Warren Buffet

指示清晰

THE LAW OF CONTEXT

THE LAW OF CONTEXT

Definitions of Context

The circumstances that form the setting for an event, statement, or idea and in terms of which it can be fully understood and assessed

The parts of something, written or spoken, that immediately precede and follow a word or passage and clarify its meaning

The Law of Context

Context is decisive.

Elements of the Law

Context is critical and conclusive.

Without context, words and actions have no power.

Context trumps strategy.

If you want to make big changes, change the context.

New problems that are solved in a new context were problems that were unsolvable in the old context.

Job one of a leader is to generate and sustain a context in which success occurs.

For me context is the key—from that comes
the understanding of everything.

—Kenneth Noland

THE LAW OF
RESPONSIBILITY

THE LAW OF RESPONSIBILITY

Definitions of Responsibility

State or fact of being responsible, answerable, or accountable for something within your power of being

An obligation upon you who is responsible

A person or thing for which one is responsible

Reliability or dependability, especially in meeting your debts, payments, and promises

The Law of Responsibility

Responsibility begins and ends with you standing for you are *cause* in the matter.

Elements of the Law of Responsibility

Responsibility displaces fault and blame.

Shame and guilt are the opposite of responsibility.

Holding yourself as responsible will give you power.

Holding yourself as responsible will make you humble.

Holding yourself as responsible will make you grow up.

Holding yourself as responsible squashes your ego.

Until you are responsible for the problem, the problem persists.

The only way to change something is be responsible for it.

Personal responsibility is not only recognizing the errors of your ways. Personal responsibility lies in your willingness and ability to correct those errors individually and collectively.

—Yehuda Berg

知己知彼

THE LAW OF
SELF-AWARENESS

THE LAW OF SELF-AWARENESS

Definitions of Self-Awareness

An awareness of one's own personality or individuality

The state or condition of being aware; having knowledge of oneself; consciousness

Good knowledge and judgment about oneself

The Law of Self-Awareness

Being self-aware enables better decisions, less reactivity, and greater connection.

Elements of the Law of Self-Awareness

Elements include intellectual and emotional understanding of yourself.

Leaders who are not self-aware don't stay leaders for very long.

You are able to recognize your strengths and weaknesses.

You are able to recognize your trigger points and how you react.

You are able to stop yourself from taking on other people's emotional baggage.

You are able to catch yourself before you do something you'll regret.

You can make far better choices.

You are able to regulate, not react.

A person who doesn't examine his or her life never changes.

> I think self-awareness is probably the most important thing towards being a champion.
>
> —Billie Jean King

男敢自信

THE LAW OF COURAGE

THE LAW OF COURAGE

Definitions of Courage

Mental or moral strength to venture, persevere, and withstand danger, fear, or difficulty

The quality of mind or spirit that enables a person to face difficulty, danger, or pain without fear; bravery

The Law of Courage

Courage is the power of *being* able to overcome fear.

Elements of the Law of Courage

No risk, no reward.

Let go of the familiar.

Be yourself in a world that wants you to be someone else.

Life either contracts or expands in relationship to your courage.

Courage is what it takes to stand up and speak.

Don't be afraid to fail.

Courage allows you to become who you really are.

Do not let your fears dominate your actions.

Success is not final; failure is not fatal: it is
the courage to continue that counts.

—Winston Churchill

核心價值明確

THE LAW OF CORE VALUES

THE LAW OF CORE VALUES

Definitions of Core Values

A principle or belief that a person or organization views as being of central importance

Those values that an individual or an organization holds that form the foundation on which they perform work and conduct themselves

The basis upon which an individual or members of a company make decisions, plan strategies, and interact with each other and their stakeholders

The Law of Core Values

Core values decide how you decide.

Element of the Law of Core Values

A company's core values define its character and brand.

Your personal core values define who you are.

Core values tell you the difference between right and wrong.

When you breach a core value, integrity weakens.

Core values are your DNA.

Core values are the person you are when no one is watching.

Core values are like fingerprints. They are your very own, and you leave them on everything you touch.

As we grow as a company, it has become more
and more important to explicitly define the
core values from which we develop our culture,
our brand and our business strategy.

—Tony Hsieh

他誠率真

THE LAW OF
AUTHENTICITY

THE LAW OF AUTHENTICITY

Definitions of Authenticity

Not false or imitation; real; actual

True to one's own personality, spirit, or character

The quality of being authentic; genuineness

The Law of Authenticity

Authenticity generates trust, gratitude, and allegiance.

Elements of the Law of Authenticity

Authenticity requires vulnerability, transparency, and integrity.

Authenticity is the expression of the true self.

Authenticity is expressing the person you really are.

Authenticity is the courage to be yourself.

Being authentic is compelling.

Don't compromise your authenticity for approval.

Authenticity is your most valuable commodity.

Dare to be yourself.

Be authentic. Be genuine.
Be real. Be yourself.

—Tai Sheridan

有的放矢

THE LAW OF
INTENTIONALITY

THE LAW OF INTENTIONALITY

Definitions of Intentionality

The state of having or being formed by an intention

The property of being about or directed toward a subject, as inherent in conscious states, beliefs, or creations of the mind

Done with intention or on purpose

The Law or Intentionality

Intentionality results in the ability to manifest.

The Elements of the Law of Intentionality

Intentionality displaces doubt.

Intentionality reshapes your perception.

Intentionality gives you the power to create.

Intentionality is required to produce change.

Intentionality streams energy into a focused force.

Intentionality alters relationship to circumstances.

Inspiration is intention followed.

The abilities of creativity when matched with the power of intentionality becomes reality.

Intentionality fuels the master's journey.

—George Leonard

高瞻遠矚

THE LAW OF VISION

THE LAW OF VISION

Definitions of Vision

An idea or mental image of something

An aspirational description of what an organization would like to achieve in the future; intended to serve as a clear guide for choosing current and future courses of action

A picture of your company in the future, which inspires and generates the framework for strategic planning

Law of Vision

Without vision, the past becomes the future.

Elements of the Law Vision

The essence of leadership is vision.

Leadership's job is converting vision into reality.

Vision requires action to manifest itself.

Fear stops vision.

A vision is a future that wasn't going to happen anyway.

Vision is possible only when you have a great team.

Don't underestimate the power of vision to change the world.

A clear vision comes from your heart, not your head.

Vision connects you but also separates you.

Good business leaders create a vision, articulate
the vision, passionately own the vision,
and relentlessly drive it to completion.

—Jack Welch

THE LAW OF PURPOSE

THE LAW OF PURPOSE

Definitions of Purpose

Something set up as an object or end to be attained

A subject under discussion or an action in course of execution

The reason for which something is done or created or for which something exists

The object toward which one strives or for which something exists; an aim or goal

The "why"

The Law of Purpose

Success occurs when people commit to a common purpose.

Elements of the Law of Purpose

Existence is not about staying alive but about finding out what to live for.

People commit not to what you do but to why you do it.

A person lacking purpose is like a boat without a rudder.

Purpose gives tenacity.

Effort is not enough without purpose.

Purpose doesn't need motivation.

Purpose provokes passion.

Keep yourself and your company on purpose.

I want to live my life in such a way that
when I get out of bed in the morning,
the devil says, "Aw shit, he's up!"

—Steve Maraboli

樂於奉獻

THE LAW OF
CONTRIBUTION

THE LAW OF CONTRIBUTION

Definition of Contribution

To give or supply in common with others

To give a part to the common good

To play a significant part in bringing about an end or result

The Law of Contribution

When you expand the focus of your company beyond profit and competition to include contribution, magic happens.

Elements of the Law of Contribution

The secret to life is giving, not getting.

Nothing you get comes close to what you can give.

The rewards in business are in direct proportion to what it contributes.

Your level of contentment is a function of the level of contribution you make.

Life's deepest reward is through selfless contribution.

A life remembered is not about accumulation but about contribution.

When you cease to make a
contribution, you begin to die.

—Eleanor Roosevelt

CONCLUSION

It's simple and direct: if you obey the twelve laws of leadership, you will become a much more powerful leader. If you rule and are ruled by these laws, you will expand your influence and reach as a leader. If you continue to own and observe these laws, you will be a leader worth following.

The qualities of a great leader are vision,
integrity, courage, understanding, the power
of articulation and profundity of character.

—President Dwight D. Eisenhower

DR. MARC B. COOPER'S  professional career includes his being a private-practice periodontist, academician, researcher, teacher, practice-management consultant, corporate consultant, trainer, seminar director, board director, author, entrepreneur, and inventor.

In his career, besides the dental industry, Dr. Cooper has worked with Silicon Valley start-ups, hospitals and hospital systems, insurance companies, and several Fortune 500 companies. Dr. Cooper has worked with dental clients in the United States, United Kingdom, Australia, Cambodia, Canada, Portugal, Italy, Greece, Dubai, Abu Dhabi, Oman, Brazil, Chile, Singapore, New Zealand, and Israel.

Today, Dr. Cooper's work is focused on leadership development and strategies to succeed in the emerging future of dentistry. Over the last six years, Dr. Cooper has worked with dentist-entrepreneurs worldwide to generate highly successful managed group practices.

Dr. Cooper has also worked in the domain of self-awareness for more than thirty years: *est*, Landmark Education, Pathworks, Neurolinguistic Programming,

Edwin Friedman, Abraham Maslow and Daniel Goleman's work on self-actualization and self-differentiation, training and therapy with a Jungian psychiatrist on individuation, and Buddhist meditation and other meditative programs at Naropa University.

Dr. Cooper is author of eight successful books: *Mastering the Business of Practice*, *Partnerships in Dental Practice*, *Running on Empty*, *SOURCE*, *Valuocity*, *Valuocity II*, *Valuocity III*, and *The Elder*. His electronic newsletter reaches thousands of subscribers in thirty-one countries. Dr. Cooper also codeveloped a suite of online dental practice management assessment tools.

For more information about the Dentist Entrepreneur Organization (DEO) and its programs, please go to www.deodentalgroup.com.

REFERENCES

1. *Wikipedia*
2. *Merriam-Webster Dictionary*
3. *Oxford Dictionary*
4. *Cambridge Dictionary*
5. *Macmillan Dictionary*
6. *Collins Dictionary*

Printed in the United States
By Bookmasters